The Witch of Blackbird Pond
Novel Literature Unit Study and Lapbook

**Unit Study Created
by Teresa Ives Lilly**

www.hshighlights.com

This unit can be used in any grade level in which students are able to read the book. The activities are best used in grades 2 to 6. Almost everything in the unit can be used to create a file folder lap book. Each unit study covers one whole book and includes:

Comprehension Activities:
Fill in the Blanks, True and False, Multiple Choice,
Who, What, Where, When, Why and How Questions.

Pre-Reading Skills Activities
Author Information Activity, Time line Activity, Theater Box Activity

Lesson Activities
Encyclopedia, Journal, Vocabulary, Sequence of Events, Handwriting
Main Idea, Key Event, Prediction, Comparison,

Literature Skills Activity
Main Character, Main Setting, Main Problem, Possible Solutions, Character Traits, Character Interaction, Cause and Effect, Description, Pyramid of Importance, Villain vs. Hero

Poetry Skills Activity
Couplet, Triplet, Quinzain, Haiku, Cinquain, Tanka, Diamanté, Lantern and Shape Poem

Newspaper Writing Activity
Editorial, Travel, Advice Column, Comics, Society News, Sports, Obituary, Weddings, Book Review, Wanted Ads, Word Search

Creative Writing Activity
Letter, Fairy Tale, Mystery, Science Fiction, Fable, Dream or Nightmare, Tall Tale, Memoir, Newberry Award, A Different Ending.

Writing Skills Activity
Description, Expository, Dialogue, Process, Point of View, Persuasion, Compare and Contrast, Sequel, Climax and Plot Analysis.

Poster Board Activity
Collage, Theater Poster, Wanted Poster, Coat of Arms, Story Quilt, Chalk Art, Silhouette, Board Game Construction, Door Sign, Jeopardy.

Art Expression Activity
Main Character, Main Setting, Travel Brochure, Postal Stamp, Book Cover, Menu, Fashion Designer, Puzzle, Mini Book, Ten Commandments.

Creative Art Activity
Sculpture, Shadow Box, Mosaic, Mobile, Acrostic, Tapestry, Paper Dolls, Book Mark, Photography, Parade Float, Sketch

Other Activities:
Sign Language Vocabulary, Literature Web, Bingo.

Published at www.hshighlights.com
Copyright © 2009 All rights reserved
Teachers may make copies for their individual students only

How to do the Lapbook Activity: To use this unit study either print out all the pages or Student wills recreate most of them in a notebook or on white or colored paper.

All of the pages can be added to the lapbook project as shown in the photos, or only use those items you want to have students create a lapbook and have them use a spiral notebook for the other pages.

The following are photos of how the work can be presented in the lapbook format. To create the lapbook use 3-6 file folders (colored are best), construction paper or index cards, markers, glue and a stapler.

Front

Back

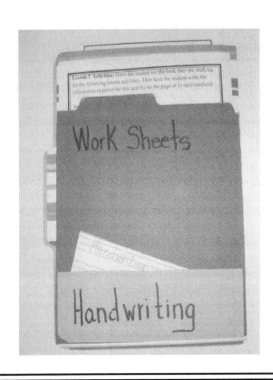

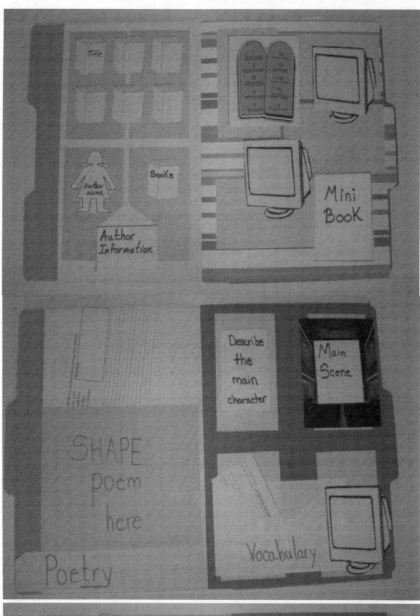
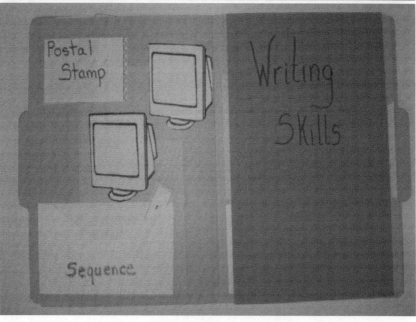

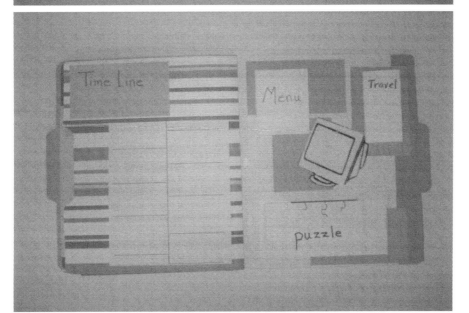

How to do the Newspaper Activity: As the student completes the news paper activities, have student lay the completed work out on a big board or on several poster boards. Don't have them glue the items on the board until the entire newspaper is completed and all sections are put where the student wants them to be. Have student create a name for their newspaper. Then have them type out the name, in big bold letters and place it on the top of the board. with tape or sticky clay. Then tape of stick all the completed articles onto board as well.

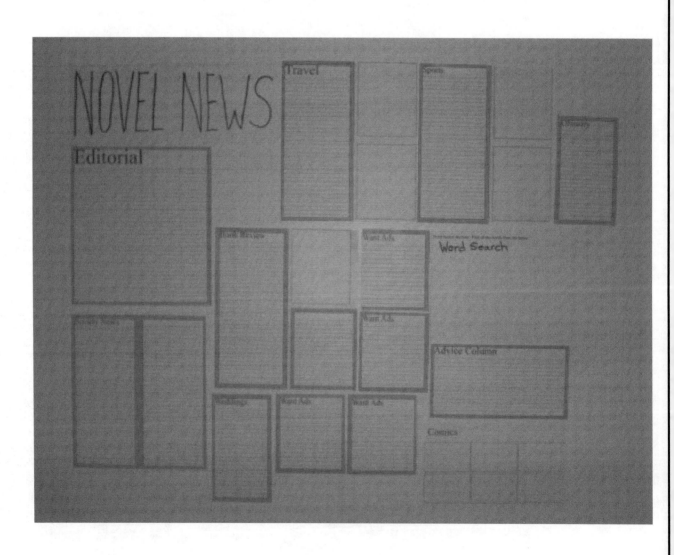

Pre-Reading Activities

Pre-Reading Activity: Student will look at the book they will be studying for this unit. Then student will write the information required for this activity on the following book patterns or in their notebook. The patterns may be cut out and placed on the lapbook.

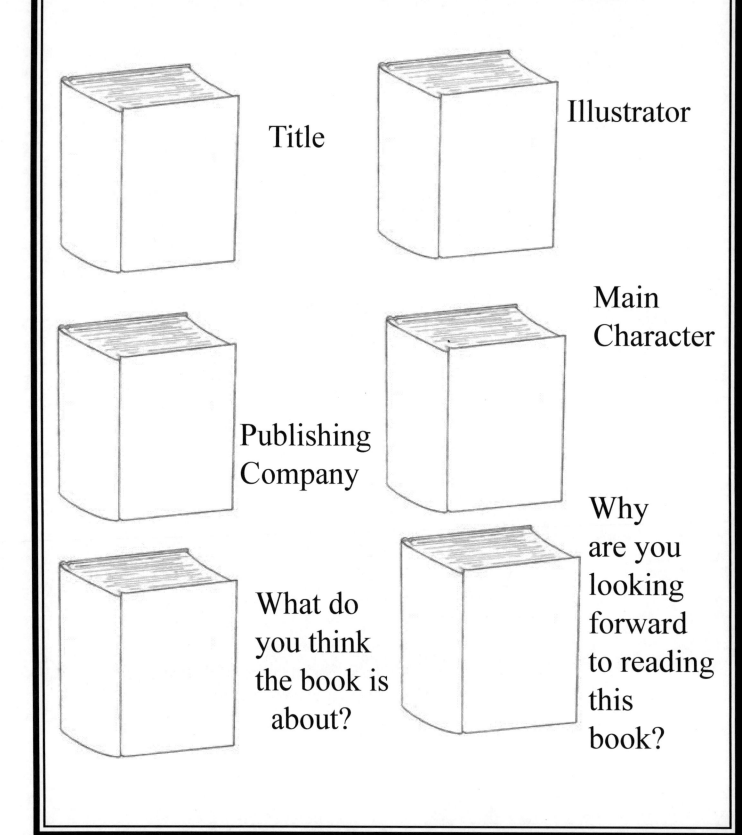

Author Activity: Student will use the book they are studying and information found on the internet to find out information about the author. Then student will write the information required for this activity on the patterns or in their notebook. The patterns may be cut out and placed on the lapbook.

Student will write the author's name on the correct pattern and the author's age.

Student will rite the name of all the books written by this author on the book pattern. If there are more than three books, just select the three most famous.

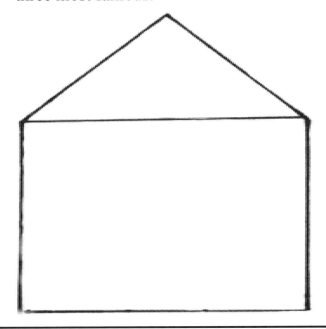

Student will write information about the author on the house pattern, such as where the author was born, lived and how they became an author.

Time Line Activity: Student will use the book they are studying to fill out the time line indicating when anything new, interesting or important happens in the book. This time line pattern can be copied into the student's notebook or this pattern can be printed smaller and placed on the lapbook.

All Vocabulary Lists, Comprehension Questions, True and False, Fill in the Blank for each lesson are at the end of this unit study.

Lesson 1
Activities

Lesson 1 Activities: Students will use the book they are studying and information found on the internet for the following activities. Then the student will write the information required for this activity on the patterns or in their notebook. The patterns may be cut out and placed on the lapbook.

Encyclopedia:
Student will choose one subject from this lesson that interested them and look it up on the internet or in encyclopedia. They will write the name of the subject across the top of the monitor pattern. On the monitor screen section, they will write three or more interesting facts about the subject.

Journal:
Student will imagine that they are one of the characters from the story. After reading each lesson, they will write a short journal entry telling what happened from that character's point of view.
Student will also draw a picture to go along with the journal entry.
At the end of the book, student will staple all the journal entries together to form a complete booklet.
They can even create a special cover for it from construction paper.

Vocabulary word: _____
Definition of the word: _____
_____
_____

Antonym of the word: _____
How many syllables does the word have? _____

Vocabulary Word: _____
Sentence using the word: _____
_____
_____

Synonym of the word: _____

Vocabulary: Student will use the vocabulary words from the list for this lesson. On one of the patterns, or on one index card they will write one vocabulary word. They should also write the definition of the word, then the Antonym and how many Syllables the word has.

On the other card, the student will write the same word. They will write a full sentence using this word and then write the Synonym of the word.

They will repeat this for all the vocabulary words in this lesson.

Place the patterns or cards in an envelope which can be glued into the student's notebook or onto the lapbook..

Sequencing: At the end of the lesson the student will write two of the main events on these two strips. Save them in an envelope which can be glued onto the lapbook or in the notebook. At the end of the book, these strips can be taken out and the student can arrange them in the correct order as they occurred in the story.

Handwriting: Student will pick their favorite sentence that they read in this lesson. Have them write the sentence in their best handwriting on this page or in their notebook.

Student will write out the answers for the following:

Main Idea: In a sentence or two, write what the main idea was of this section.

___

Key Event: In a sentence or two write what the most important event was in this section.

___

Prediction: In a sentence of two write what you Predict will happen in the next section.

___

Comparison: In a sentence of two compare two things in this section. Tell what makes them alike and what makes them different.

___

Fact or Opinion: In one sentence write a fact about this section and one sentence that is an opinion about the lesson.

___

Literature Skills: Main Character: Student will write words in the circles to describe the main character.

Physical appearance

Concern or worry

Main character

Who they relate to

Your opinion of them

Poetry Form: Student will write a poem about the book or characters using this format.
Couplet: A Couplet is a two line poem with a fun and simple rhyming pattern. Each line has the same number of syllables and their endings must rhyme with one another. Humor is often used in couplets.

Example:
    If a seed could have its way
    it would grow in just one day.

Newspaper Activity: Student will use this form to write their newspaper piece on then paste it onto their newspaper lay out poster.

Editorial: An editorial is written by the editor of the newspaper. In an editorial the editor gives an opinion of something. Student will imagine that they are the editor of their newspaper. Student will write their opinion of something that happened in the book so far.

Editorial

Creative Writing Activity: Student will use this form or write in their notebook.
Letter Writing: Student will write a letter from one character in the book to another character in the book.

Dear   ,

Sincerely,

Writing Skills Activity: Student will use this form or write in their notebook.

Descriptive: Descriptive writing uses words such as color and texture to describe something. Student will describe a person, place or thing from the lesson.

Lapbook Activity: Main Character: Student will draw and color a picture of the main character on the solid section of the flap book. Student will cut out the entire flap book on the dotted lines and fold the four flap sections over the picture of the main character. On the outside of each flap student will write different words that describes the character; one word per flap.

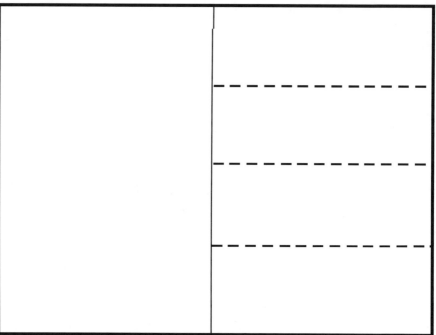

Poster Board Activity:
Book Collage
Student will print out pictures from the internet that represent characters from the story. They can use magazine pictures as well. Then student will glue these pictures all over a 1/2 poster board in an over lapping fashion to create a book collage.

Creative Art Activity:
Sculpting
Student will create on of the characters from the story out of clay or play doe.

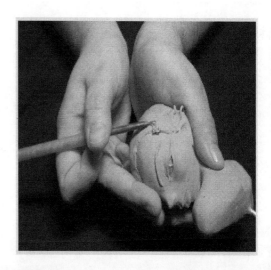

Lesson 2
Activities

Lesson 2 Activities: Students will use the book they are studying and information found on the internet for the following activities. Then the student will write the information required for this activity on the patterns or in their notebook. The patterns may be cut out and placed on the lapbook.

Encyclopedia:
Student will choose one subject from this lesson that interested them and look it up on the internet or in encyclopedia. They will write the name of the subject across the top of the monitor pattern. On the monitor screen section, they will write three or more interesting facts about the subject.

Journal:
Student will imagine that they are one of the characters from the story. After reading each lesson, they will write a short journal entry telling what happened from that character's point of view.
Student will also draw a picture to go along with the journal entry.
At the end of the book, student will staple all the journal entries together to form a complete booklet.
They can even create a special cover for it from construction paper.

Vocabulary word: _____
Definition of the word: _____
_____
_____

Antonym of the word: _____
How many syllables does the word have? _____

Vocabulary Word: _____
Sentence using the word: _____
_____
_____

Synonym of the word: _____

Vocabulary: Student will use the vocabulary words from the list for this lesson. On one of the patterns, or on one index card they will write one vocabulary word. They should also write the definition of the word, then the Antonym and how many Syllables the word has.

On the other card, the student will write the same word. They will write a full sentence using this word and then write the Synonym of the word.

They will repeat this for all the vocabulary words in this lesson.

Place the patterns or cards in an envelope which can be glued into the student's notebook or onto the lapbook..

Sequencing: At the end of the lesson the student will write two of the main events on these two strips. Save them in an envelope which can be glued onto the lapbook or in the notebook. At the end of the book, these strips can be taken out and the student can arrange them in the correct order as they occurred in the story.

Handwriting: Student will pick their favorite sentence that they read in this lesson. Have them write the sentence in their best handwriting on this page or in their notebook.

Student will write out the answers for the following:

Main Idea: In a sentence or two, write what the main idea was of this section.

Key Event: In a sentence or two write what the most important event was in this section.

Prediction: In a sentence of two write what you Predict will happen in the next section.

Comparison: In a sentence of two compare two things in this section. Tell what makes them alike and what makes them different.

Fact or Opinion: In one sentence write a fact about this section and one sentence that is an opinion about the lesson.

Main Setting: Student will fill in the information to describe the main setting and to describe the minor settings in the story.

What is the main setting? _____
_____

Describe it _____
_____
_____
_____

Describe a Minor Setting
_____
_____
_____

Describe a Minor Setting
_____
_____
_____

Poetry Form: Student will write a poem about the book or characters using this format.

Triplet:
Triplets are three-lined poems that rhyme. Each line has the same number of Syllables.

Example:
    The bunny hops and hops
    Til all at once she stops
    To munch some carrot tops.

_____
_____
_____
_____
_____
_____

Newspaper Activity: Student will use this form to write their newspaper piece on then paste it onto their newspaper lay out poster.

Travel Section: Student should imagine they write the travel column for a newspaper. Student should write a short article about traveling to the area where this book takes place. Student should find one or two photos on the internet that reminds them of this place and place it on the newspaper lay out poster as well.

Travel

Creative Writing Activity: Student will use this form or write in their notebook.

Fairy Tales : Fairy Tales are fanciful tales of legendary deeds and creatures, usually intended for children. Student will write a fairy tale involving one of the characters from the story and illustrate it.

Writing Skills Activity: Student will use this form or write in their notebook.

Persuasion: Persuasion is a way of writing, in which you convince someone of something. Student will write to try to persuade someone in the story to do something differently than they did in the story.

Lapbook Activity: Main Setting : Student will draw and color the main scene or main setting of this story for a play in this stage scene. Place in lapbook.

Poster Board Activity:
Theater Poster
Student will create a poster that may be found outside of a theater which is putting on a play of this book.

Creative Art Activity:
Shadow Box:
Student will use a shoe box turned on its side to create a scene from the book in using pictures from the internet or other small items.

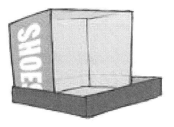

Lesson 3
Activities

Lesson 3 Activities: Students will use the book they are studying and information found on the internet for the following activities. Then the student will write the information required for this activity on the patterns or in their notebook. The patterns may be cut out and placed on the lapbook.

Encyclopedia:
Student will choose one subject from this lesson that interested them and look it up on the internet or in encyclopedia. They will write the name of the subject across the top of the monitor pattern. On the monitor screen section, they will write three or more interesting facts about the subject.

Journal:
Student will imagine that they are one of the characters from the story. After reading each lesson, they will write a short journal entry telling what happened from that character's point of view.
Student will also draw a picture to go along with the journal entry.
At the end of the book, student will staple all the journal entries together to form a complete booklet.
They can even create a special cover for it from construction paper.

Vocabulary word: _____
Definition of the word: _____
_____
_____

Antonym of the word: _____
How many syllables does the word have? _____

Vocabulary Word: _____
Sentence using the word: _____
_____
_____

Synonym of the word: _____

Vocabulary: Student will use the vocabulary words from the list for this lesson. On one of the patterns, or on one index card they will write one vocabulary word. They should also write the definition of the word, then the Antonym and how many Syllables the word has.

On the other card, the student will write the same word. They will write a full sentence using this word and then write the Synonym of the word.

They will repeat this for all the vocabulary words in this lesson.

Place the patterns or cards in an envelope which can be glued into the student's notebook or onto the lapbook..

Sequencing: At the end of the lesson the student will write two of the main events on these two strips. Save them in an envelope which can be glued onto the lapbook or in the notebook. At the end of the book, these strips can be taken out and the student can arrange them in the correct order as they occurred in the story.

Handwriting: Student will pick their favorite sentence that they read in this lesson. Have them write the sentence in their best handwriting on this page or in their notebook.

Student will write out the answers for the following:

Main Idea: In a sentence or two, write what the main idea was of this section.

_____
_____
_____
_____
_____
_____

Key Event: In a sentence or two write what the most important event was in this section.

_____
_____
_____
_____
_____
_____
_____

Prediction: In a sentence of two write what you Predict will happen in the next section.

_____
_____
_____
_____
_____
_____
_____

Comparison: In a sentence of two compare two things in this section. Tell what makes them alike and what makes them different.

_____
_____
_____
_____
_____
_____

Fact or Opinion: In one sentence write a fact about this section and one sentence that is an opinion about the lesson.

_____
_____
_____
_____
_____
_____

Main Problem: Most stories seem to have one main problem. There may be other small problems, but there is an overall large problem. Student will write what the main problem is in the larger rectangle, and some of the smaller problems in the smaller ones.

Poetry Form: Student will write a poem about the book or characters using this format.

Quinzain: Quinzains are unrhymed three line poems that contain 15 syllables. The pattern is: The first line is 7, the second is 5 and the third is 3. The first line makes a statement and the next two lines ask a question about the subject.

Example:
> I like to write poetry
> would you like to write
> a poem too?

Newspaper Activity: Student will use this form to write their newspaper piece on then paste it onto their newspaper lay out poster.

Wanted Ads Section: Student will create several wanted ads that characters in the story might post in a newspaper or ads the characters might answer.

Creative Writing Activity: Student will use this form or write in their notebook.

Mystery: Student will write a mystery that may occur in this story or to the characters in this story and then illustrate it.

Writing Skills Activity: Student will use this form or write in their notebook.

Expository: Expository writing is writing strictly to inform. Student will write an expository piece that informs someone about an event that happened in the story.

Lapbook Activity: Travel Brochure: Student will use this form to create a travel brochure on. It should describe a place in the story that people should come to visit. Student may use pictures from the internet if necessary.

Poster Board Activity:
Wanted Poster
Student will create a "Wanted by the Law," poster for one of the villains in the story.

Creative Art Activity:
Mosaic Plate
Student will create a mosaic scene from the story on a paper plate using small pieces of construction paper glued in a mosaic fashion.

Lesson 4
Activities

Lesson 4 Activities: Students will use the book they are studying and information found on the internet for the following activities. Then the student will write the information required for this activity on the patterns or in their notebook. The patterns may be cut out and placed on the lapbook.

Encyclopedia:
Student will choose one subject from this lesson that interested them and look it up on the internet or in encyclopedia. They will write the name of the subject across the top of the monitor pattern. On the monitor screen section, they will write three or more interesting facts about the subject.

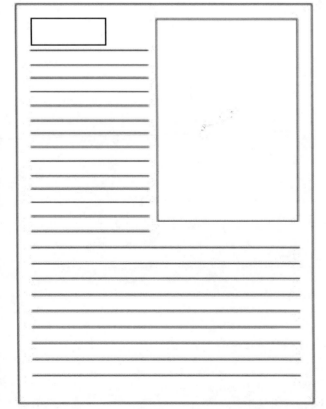

Journal:
Student will imagine that they are one of the characters from the story. After reading each lesson, they will write a short journal entry telling what happened from that character's point of view.
Student will also draw a picture to go along with the journal entry.
At the end of the book, student will staple all the journal entries together to form a complete booklet.
They can even create a special cover for it from construction paper.

Vocabulary word: _____
Definition of the word: _____
_____
_____

Antonym of the word: _____
How many syllables does the word have? _____

Vocabulary Word: _____
Sentence using the word: _____
_____
_____

Synonym of the word: _____

Vocabulary: Student will use the vocabulary words from the list for this lesson. On one of the patterns, or on one index card they will write one vocabulary word. They should also write the definition of the word, then the Antonym and how many Syllables the word has.

On the other card, the student will write the same word. They will write a full sentence using this word and then write the Synonym of the word.

They will repeat this for all the vocabulary words in this lesson.

Place the patterns or cards in an envelope which can be glued into the student's notebook or onto the lapbook..

Sequencing: At the end of the lesson the student will write two of the main events on these two strips. Save them in an envelope which can be glued onto the lapbook or in the notebook. At the end of the book, these strips can be taken out and the student can arrange them in the correct order as they occurred in the story.

Handwriting: Student will pick their favorite sentence that they read in this lesson. Have them write the sentence in their best handwriting on this page or in their notebook.

Student will write out the answers for the following:

Main Idea: In a sentence or two, write what the main idea was of this section.

_____
_____
_____
_____
_____

Key Event: In a sentence or two write what the most important event was in this section.

_____
_____
_____
_____
_____

Prediction: In a sentence of two write what you Predict will happen in the next section.

_____
_____
_____
_____
_____

Comparison: In a sentence of two compare two things in this section. Tell what makes them alike and what makes them different.

_____
_____
_____
_____
_____

Fact or Opinion: In one sentence write a fact about this section and one sentence that is an opinion about the lesson.

_____
_____
_____
_____
_____

Possible Solutions: Problems in a story can have several solutions. Student will write what some of the problems are in the story and possible solution in the shapes.

Problem:

Solution:

Problem:

Solution:

Problem:

Solution:

Poetry Form: Student will write a poem about the book or characters using this format.

Haiku: A haiku is a Japanese poem with no rhyme. Haiku poems have only three lines, each with a certain number of syllables.

Here is the pattern:
Line 1 = 5 syllables
Line 2 = 7 syllables
Line 3 = 5 syllables

Example:
Lion cubs doze in
shade, under shrubs, hidden from
hungry hyenas

Newspaper Activity: Student will use this form to write their newspaper piece on then paste it onto their newspaper lay out poster.

Advice Column Section: Student will come up with a question or concern that one of the characters in the story may have. The student will write a letter to the advice column and the advice column writer will answer.

Advice Column

Creative Writing Activity: Student will use this form or write in their notebook.

Science Fiction: Science Fiction stories take place in the far future usually in space or on earth in an advanced society. Student will write a science fiction story about the future of one of the characters and illustrate it.

Writing Skills Activity: Student will use this form or write in their notebook.

Dialogue: A dialogue is a conversation between two characters. Student will write a dialogue that could occur between two characters in the story. Student should use correct quotation marks.

Writing Skills Activity: Student will use this form or write in their notebook.

Lapbook Activity: Postal Stamp: Student will create a new postal stamp for next year which would represent the book or characters of the book.

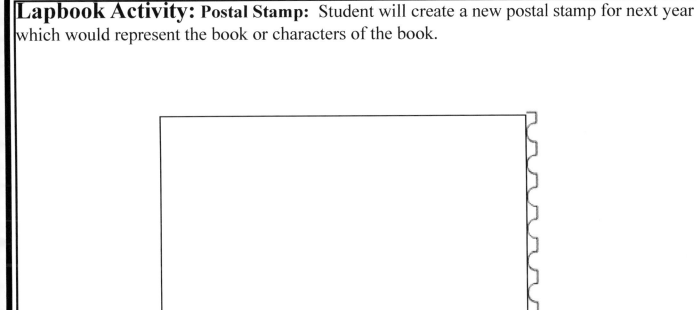

Poster Board Activity:
Coat of Arms
Using a poster board, student will create a coat of arms with a design to represent this story or a character in the story.

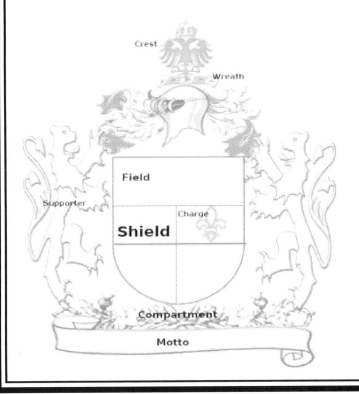

Creative Art Activity:
Mobile
Student will cut out pictures from the internet of characters of items that represent those in the book and then glue them onto long strips of card board. These can be hung with string to make a mobile.

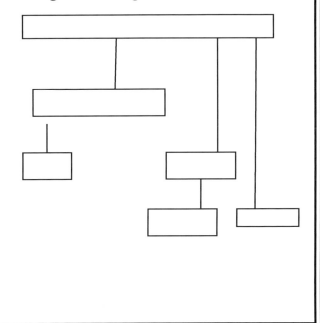

Lesson 5
Activities

Lesson 5 Activities: Students will use the book they are studying and information found on the internet for the following activities. Then the student will write the information required for this activity on the patterns or in their notebook. The patterns may be cut out and placed on the lapbook.

Encyclopedia:
Student will choose one subject from this lesson that interested them and look it up on the internet or in encyclopedia. They will write the name of the subject across the top of the monitor pattern. On the monitor screen section, they will write three or more interesting facts about the subject.

Journal:
Student will imagine that they are one of the characters from the story. After reading each lesson, they will write a short journal entry telling what happened from that character's point of view.
Student will also draw a picture to go along with the journal entry.
At the end of the book, student will staple all the journal entries together to form a complete booklet.
They can even create a special cover for it from construction paper.

Vocabulary word: _____
Definition of the word: _____
_____
_____

Antonym of the word: _____
How many syllables does the word have? _____

Vocabulary Word: _____
Sentence using the word: _____
_____
_____

Synonym of the word: _____

Vocabulary: Student will use the vocabulary words from the list for this lesson. On one of the patterns, or on one index card they will write one vocabulary word. They should also write the definition of the word, then the Antonym and how many Syllables the word has.

On the other card, the student will write the same word. They will write a full sentence using this word and then write the Synonym of the word.

They will repeat this for all the vocabulary words in this lesson.

Place the patterns or cards in an envelope which can be glued into the student's notebook or onto the lapbook..

Sequencing: At the end of the lesson the student will write two of the main events on these two strips. Save them in an envelope which can be glued onto the lapbook or in the notebook. At the end of the book, these strips can be taken out and the student can arrange them in the correct order as they occurred in the story.

Handwriting: Student will pick their favorite sentence that they read in this lesson. Have them write the sentence in their best handwriting on this page or in their notebook.

Student will write out the answers for the following:

Main Idea: In a sentence or two, write what the main idea was of this section.

Key Event: In a sentence or two write what the most important event was in this section.

Prediction: In a sentence of two write what you Predict will happen in the next section.

Comparison: In a sentence of two compare two things in this section. Tell what makes them alike and what makes them different.

Fact or Opinion: In one sentence write a fact about this section and one sentence that is an opinion about the lesson.

Character Traits: In the circle for the Main Character Traits, student will write several of the main character's traits. In the circle for Student Traits, student will write several of the student's traits. Any traits that the main character and the student have in common should be in the area where the circles overlap called Common Traits.

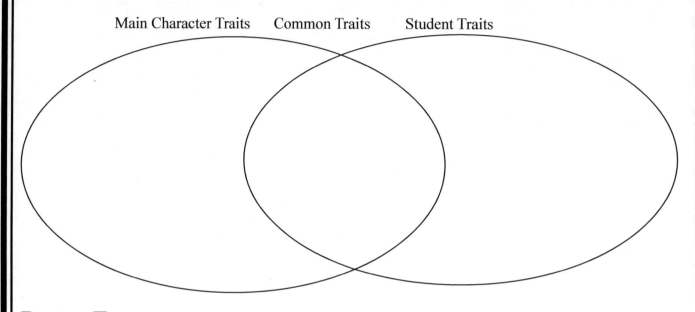

Main Character Traits   Common Traits   Student Traits

Poetry Form: Student will write a poem about the book or characters using this format.

Acrostic: In an acrostic poem the name of the person, object, or place is written vertically down the left hand side of the page. Each letter is capitalized and becomes the first letter of the word beginning each line. The words used should describe the person, object or place in a positive way. Each line may comprise a word, a phrase or a thought that is continued on to the next line.

Example:
    CAT
Can you see their eyes
At night in the dark
They glow........

_____
_____
_____
_____
_____
_____
_____
_____
_____
_____
_____
_____

Newspaper Activity: Student will use this form to write their newspaper piece on then paste it onto their newspaper lay out poster.

Comic Section: Student will create a funny cartoon about one of the events of characters in the story. Illustrate and color it.

Comics

Creative Writing Activity: Student will use this form or write in their notebook.
Fable: A fable is a short, allegorical narrative, making a moral point, traditionally by means of animal characters that speak and act like humans. Student will write a fable that comes to mind while reading this story in which one of the characters from the book learns a moral from an animal. Then student will illustrate it.

Writing Skills Activity: Student will use this form or write in their notebook.

Process: Process writing is telling the actual steps it takes to do something. Student will write a step by step process that one of the characters in the book had to do to or should have done.

Lapbook Activity: Book Cover Illustrator: Student will create their own book cover for this story on the form. Make sure to include the title, illustrator and publisher's name.

Poster Board Activity:
Story Quilt
Divide a poster board into eight to sixteen equal squares. In each square the student will draw different pictures to tell what has happened in the story so far.

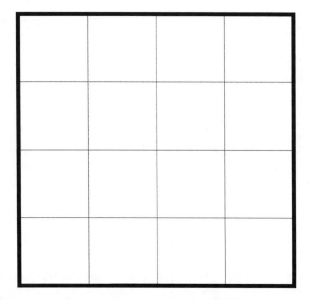

Creative Art Activity:
Tapestry
Using an 8 inch by 12 inch piece of felt as the background, student will cut out characters and items from the story from colored felt and glue onto the background to create a story tapestry.

Lesson 6
Activities

Lesson 6 Activities: Students will use the book they are studying and information found on the internet for the following activities. Then the student will write the information required for this activity on the patterns or in their notebook. The patterns may be cut out and placed on the lapbook.

Encyclopedia:
Student will choose one subject from this lesson that interested them and look it up on the internet or in encyclopedia. They will write the name of the subject across the top of the monitor pattern. On the monitor screen section, they will write three or more interesting facts about the subject.

Journal:
Student will imagine that they are one of the characters from the story. After reading each lesson, they will write a short journal entry telling what happened from that character's point of view.
Student will also draw a picture to go along with the journal entry.
At the end of the book, student will staple all the journal entries together to form a complete booklet.
They can even create a special cover for it from construction paper.

Vocabulary word: _____
Definition of the word: _____
_____
_____

Antonym of the word: _____
How many syllables does the word have? _____

Vocabulary Word: _____
Sentence using the word: _____
_____
_____

Synonym of the word: _____

Vocabulary: Student will use the vocabulary words from the list for this lesson. On one of the patterns, or on one index card they will write one vocabulary word. They should also write the definition of the word, then the Antonym and how many Syllables the word has.

On the other card, the student will write the same word. They will write a full sentence using this word and then write the Synonym of the word.

They will repeat this for all the vocabulary words in this lesson.

Place the patterns or cards in an envelope which can be glued into the student's notebook or onto the lapbook..

Sequencing: At the end of the lesson the student will write two of the main events on these two strips. Save them in an envelope which can be glued onto the lapbook or in the notebook. At the end of the book, these strips can be taken out and the student can arrange them in the correct order as they occurred in the story.

Handwriting: Student will pick their favorite sentence they read in this lesson. Have them write the sentence in their best handwriting on this page or in their notebook.

Student will write out the answers for the following:

Main Idea: In a sentence or two, write what the main idea was of this section.

_____
_____
_____
_____
_____

Key Event: In a sentence or two write what the most important event was in this section.

_____
_____
_____
_____
_____

Prediction: In a sentence of two write what you Predict will happen in the next section.

_____
_____
_____
_____
_____

Comparison: In a sentence of two compare two things in this section. Tell what makes them alike and what makes them different.

_____
_____
_____
_____
_____

Fact or Opinion: In one sentence write a fact about this section and one sentence that is an opinion about the lesson.

_____
_____
_____
_____
_____

Character Interaction: In the circles, student will write the names of the characters in the story and then draw arrows from each circle to other circles to represent which character interact with one another. Start with the Main Character in the center.

Poetry Form: Student will write a poem about the book or characters using this format.

Cinquain: A cinquain is a short, five-line, non rhyming poem which follows the following pattern:

First line - The title (one word)
2nd line - Describes the title (two words)
3rd line - Express action (three words)
4th line - A feeling or thought (four words)
5th line - A Synonym or close word for the title

Example:
Insect
six legs
usually have wings
a mostly helpful annoyance
Bee

Newspaper Activity: Student will use this form to write their newspaper piece on then paste it onto their newspaper lay out poster.

Obituary Section: Student will imagine that one or more of the characters in the book died and will write an obituary telling how they died.

Wedding Announcement Section: Student will imagine that one of the characters in the story will get married soon and will write the wedding announcement, telling who they will marry, where and when the wedding will take place.

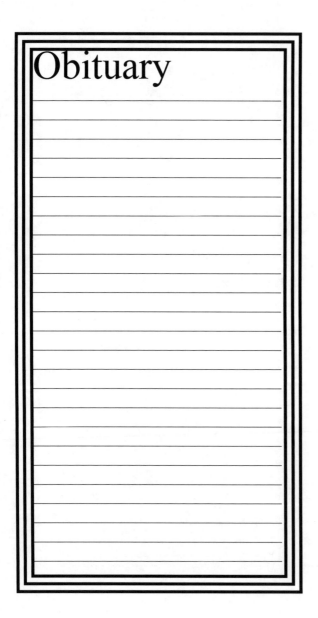
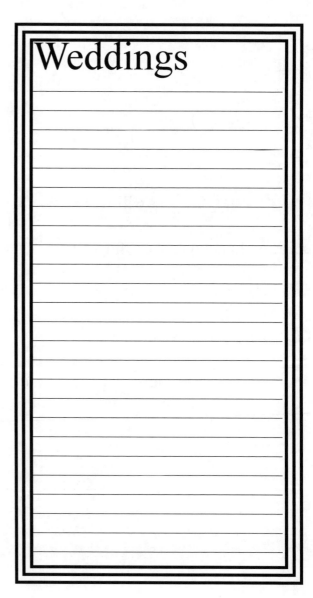

Creative Writing Activity: Dream or Nightmare: Student will write a dream or nightmare one of the characters in the story may have, and illustrate it.

Writing Skills Activity: Student will use this form or write in their notebook.

Point of View: Point of View is telling a story from one person's view. Student will write about an event in this story from a different character's point of view.

Lapbook Activity: Menu: Student will create a menu for a restaurant that the characters in the book may have owned or eaten at. Student will decorate the front of the menu in an interesting and inviting fashion.

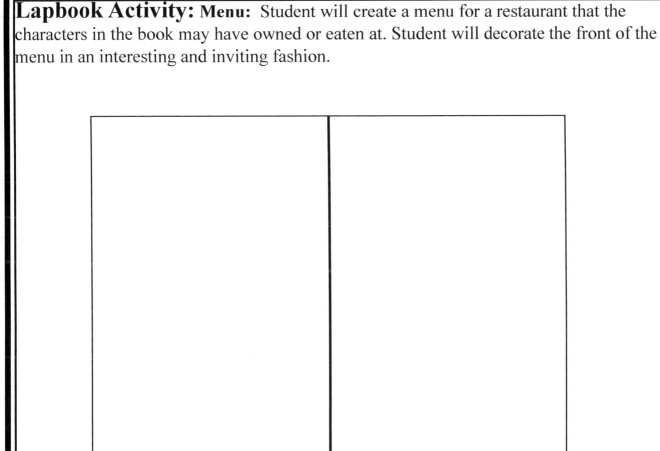

Poster Board Activity:
Chalk Art
On a black poster board student will use colored chalk to illustrate a scene or event in the story.

Creative Art Activity:
Paper Doll
Student will cut out pictures from the internet of people to represent the characters in this story and then laminate them and glue them onto sticks. Students can use them to act out parts of the story or the dialogue the student wrote in an earlier lesson.

Lesson 7
Activities

Lesson 7 Activities: Students will use the book they are studying and information found on the internet for the following activities. Then the student will write the information required for this activity on the patterns or in their notebook. The patterns may be cut out and placed on the lapbook.

Encyclopedia:
Student will choose one subject from this lesson that interested them and look it up on the internet or in encyclopedia. They will write the name of the subject across the top of the monitor pattern. On the monitor screen section, they will write three or more interesting facts about the subject.

Journal:
Student will imagine that they are one of the characters from the story. After reading each lesson, they will write a short journal entry telling what happened from that character's point of view.
Student will also draw a picture to go along with the journal entry.
At the end of the book, student will staple all the journal entries together to form a complete booklet.
They can even create a special cover for it from construction paper.

Vocabulary word: _____
Definition of the word: _____
_____
_____

Antonym of the word: _____
How many syllables does the word have? _____

Vocabulary Word: _____
Sentence using the word: _____
_____
_____

Synonym of the word: _____

Vocabulary: Student will use the vocabulary words from the list for this lesson. On one of the patterns, or on one index card they will write one vocabulary word. They should also write the definition of the word, then the Antonym and how many Syllables the word has.

On the other card, the student will write the same word. They will write a full sentence using this word and then write the Synonym of the word.

They will repeat this for all the vocabulary words in this lesson.

Place the patterns or cards in an envelope which can be glued into the student's notebook or onto the lapbook..

Sequencing: At the end of the lesson the student will write two of the main events on these two strips. Save them in an envelope which can be glued onto the lapbook or in the notebook. At the end of the book, these strips can be taken out and the student can arrange them in the correct order as they occurred in the story.

Handwriting: Student will pick their favorite sentence that they read in this lesson. Have them write the sentence in their best handwriting on this page or in their notebook.

Student will write out the answers for the following:

Main Idea: In a sentence or two, write what the main idea was of this section.

_____
_____
_____
_____
_____
_____

Key Event: In a sentence or two write what the most important event was in this section.

_____
_____
_____
_____
_____
_____

Prediction: In a sentence of two write what you Predict will happen in the next section.

_____
_____
_____
_____
_____
_____

Comparison: In a sentence of two compare two things in this section. Tell what makes them alike and what makes them different.

_____
_____
_____
_____
_____

Fact or Opinion: In one sentence write a fact about this section and one sentence that is an opinion about the lesson.

_____
_____
_____
_____
_____
_____

Cause and Effect: When one thing happens in a story, many other things happen because of this one event. This is called cause and effect. In the center circle, student will write one thing that happened in the story (the cause). In the smaller circles, student will write the variety of things that happened because of that main cause (the effects).

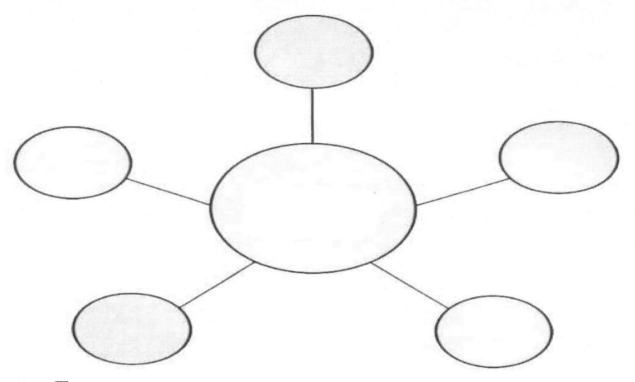

Poetry Form: Student will write a poem about the book or characters using this format.

Tanka: A Tanka is a form of Japanese poetry that depends on the number of lines and syllables instead of rhyme. The pattern is:
Line 1 = 5 syllables, Line 2 = 7 syllables
Line 3 = 5 syllables, Line 4 = 7 syllables
Line 5 = 7 syllables

Example:
Blue-eyed baby cubs
wobble out of winter's den
warm sun on cold fur
forest smells of fresh, cold pine
wild, new world to grow into.

_____
_____
_____
_____
_____
_____
_____
_____
_____
_____

Newspaper Activity: Student will use this form to write their newspaper piece on then paste it onto their newspaper lay out poster.

Society News Section: Student will write about someone in the story who would be considered a fairly famous person or character. Write a society column about an event or party that they may have attended.

Creative Writing Activity: **Tall Tale**s: Tall tales are humorous, exaggerated stories common on the American frontier. Student will write a tall tale about one of the characters in the story and then illustrate it.

Writing Skills Activity: Student will use this form or write in their notebook.

Compare and Contrast: Compare and Contrast tell about two or more things and how they are alike or different. Student will write to Compare and Contrast two characters in the story.

Lapbook Activity: Fashion Designer: Student will design clothing that one or more of the characters in the story would have worn. Student will color them or cut them out of scraps of material and put them on the doll form that represents the character and then attach to lapbook.

Poster Board Activity:
Silhouette
Using black construction paper, student will cut out a silhouette of the main character or an item from the story and glue it onto the center of a white or colored 1/2 poster board. Then student will create a frame around the outside with a black poster board.

Creative Art Activity:
Book Mark
Using thick tag board, student will cut into a rectangle 3 inches by 6 inches, and create a book mark that resembles something about the book. Then student will punch a hole in the end and tie ribbon or string through it. Laminate it if possible.

Lesson 8
Activities

Lesson 8 Activities: Students will use the book they are studying and information found on the internet for the following activities. Then the student will write the information required for this activity on the patterns or in their notebook. The patterns may be cut out and placed on the lapbook.

Encyclopedia:
Student will choose one subject from this lesson that interested them and look it up on the internet or in encyclopedia. They will write the name of the subject across the top of the monitor pattern. On the monitor screen section, they will write three or more interesting facts about the subject.

Journal:
Student will imagine that they are one of the characters from the story. After reading each lesson, they will write a short journal entry telling what happened from that character's point of view.
Student will also draw a picture to go along with the journal entry.
At the end of the book, student will staple all the journal entries together to form a complete booklet.
They can even create a special cover for it from construction paper.

Vocabulary word: _____
Definition of the word: _____
_____
_____

Antonym of the word: _____
How many syllables does the word have? _____

Vocabulary Word: _____
Sentence using the word: _____
_____
_____

Synonym of the word: _____

Vocabulary: Student will use the vocabulary words from the list for this lesson. On one of the patterns, or on one index card they will write one vocabulary word. They should also write the definition of the word, then the Antonym and how many Syllables the word has.

On the other card, the student will write the same word. They will write a full sentence using this word and then write the Synonym of the word.

They will repeat this for all the vocabulary words in this lesson.

Place the patterns or cards in an envelope which can be glued into the student's notebook or onto the lapbook..

Sequencing: At the end of the lesson the student will write two of the main events on these two strips. Save them in an envelope which can be glued onto the lapbook or in the notebook. At the end of the book, these strips can be taken out and the student can arrange them in the correct order as they occurred in the story.

Handwriting: Student will pick their favorite sentence that they read in this lesson. Have them write the sentence in their best handwriting on this page or in their notebook.

Student will write out the answers for the following:
Main Idea: In a sentence or two, write what the main idea was of this section.
_____
_____
_____
_____
_____
_____

Key Event: In a sentence or two write what the most important event was in this section.
_____
_____
_____
_____
_____
_____

Prediction: In a sentence of two write what you Predict will happen in the next section.
_____
_____
_____
_____
_____
_____

Comparison: In a sentence of two compare two things in this section. Tell what makes them alike and what makes them different.
_____
_____
_____
_____
_____
_____

Fact or Opinion: In one sentence write a fact about this section and one sentence that is an opinion about the lesson.
_____
_____
_____
_____
_____

Descriptions: Authors use descriptive words so that the reader can imagine the place or thing that is being described. Student will find one place in the book that the author really described well and write the name of the place inside the polygon. On the lines coming out of the polygon, student will write the words the author used to describe the place such as pretty, dark, blue....

Poetry Form: Student will write a poem about the book or characters using this format.

Diamanté: A diamanté is a seven-line, diamond-shaped poem which contrasts two opposites. The pattern is: First Line and seventh line - Name the opposites. Second and sixth lines - Two adjectives describing the opposite nearest it. Third and fifth lines - Three participles (ing words) describing the nearest opposite.
 Fourth line - two nouns for each of the opposites.

Example:
Fish
silvered, baited
teeming, swimming, darting
scaled amphibian, graceful hind
running, leaping, grazing
hunted, mammal
Deer

Newspaper Activity: Student will use this form to write their newspaper piece on then paste it onto their newspaper lay out poster.

Sports Section: Student will imagine that one of the characters in your book is in a sports competition and write a newspaper article about it and then illustrate it as well.

Sports

Creative Writing Activity: Memoir: When writing a memoir, a person chooses one time or one event and expounds upon it by stretching the truth. Student will write a memoir as if they were a character in the story. They should choose one event to write about, and stretch the truth in the retelling.

My Memoir

Writing Skills Activity: Student will use this form or write in their notebook.

Sequel: A sequel is a movie or book that follows another. The sequel contains the same characters and follows the same story line. The characters and story line may change during the sequel but they have to start out the same to show the connection with the previous story. Students will write the first few paragraphs of a sequel for this story.

Writing Skills Activity: Student will use this form or write in their notebook.

Lapbook Activity: **Book Cover Puzzle:** Student will glue a picture they print from the internet of the book cover, onto this puzzle pattern so that the pattern shows on the back. Then student will cut the book cover into puzzle pieces. This can go in an envelope on the lapbook to be put together later.

Poster Board Activity:
Board Game
Student will create a board game on the poster board to use with this story.

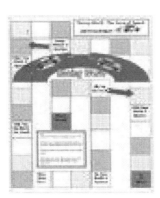

Creative Art Activity:
Photography
Photography is a great form of art. Student will find things that reminds them of this book and take some photos of it. Get these printed in black and white and some in color. Student can turn these into cards, frame them or take photos of one item in different angles and create a unique photo like this one.

Lesson 9
Activity

Lesson 9 Activities: Students will use the book they are studying and information found on the internet for the following activities. Then the student will write the information required for this activity on the patterns or in their notebook. The patterns may be cut out and placed on the lapbook.

Encyclopedia:
Student will choose one subject from this lesson that interested them and look it up on the internet or in encyclopedia. They will write the name of the subject across the top of the monitor pattern. On the monitor screen section, they will write three or more interesting facts about the subject.

Journal:
Student will imagine that they are one of the characters from the story. After reading each lesson, they will write a short journal entry telling what happened from that character's point of view.
Student will also draw a picture to go along with the journal entry.
At the end of the book, student will staple all the journal entries together to form a complete booklet.
They can even create a special cover for it from construction paper.

Vocabulary word: _____
Definition of the word: _____
_____
_____

Antonym of the word: _____
How many syllables does the word have? _____

Vocabulary Word: _____
Sentence using the word: _____
_____
_____

Synonym of the word: _____

Vocabulary: Student will use the vocabulary words from the list for this lesson. On one of the patterns, or on one index card they will write one vocabulary word. They should also write the definition of the word, then the Antonym and how many Syllables the word has.

On the other card, the student will write the same word. They will write a full sentence using this word and then write the Synonym of the word.

They will repeat this for all the vocabulary words in this lesson.

Place the patterns or cards in an envelope which can be glued into the student's notebook or onto the lapbook..

Sequencing: At the end of the lesson the student will write two of the main events on these two strips. Save them in an envelope which can be glued onto the lapbook or in the notebook. At the end of the book, these strips can be taken out and the student can arrange them in the correct order as they occurred in the story.

Handwriting: Student will pick their favorite sentence that they read in this lesson. Have them write the sentence in their best handwriting on this page or in their notebook.

Student will write out the answers for the following:

Main Idea: In a sentence or two, write what the main idea was of this section.

_____
_____
_____
_____
_____

Key Event: In a sentence or two write what the most important event was in this section.

_____
_____
_____
_____
_____
_____

Prediction: In a sentence of two write what you Predict will happen in the next section.

_____
_____
_____
_____
_____
_____

Comparison: In a sentence of two compare two things in this section. Tell what makes them alike and what makes them different.

_____
_____
_____
_____
_____
_____

Fact or Opinion: In one sentence write a fact about this section and one sentence that is an opinion about the lesson.

_____
_____
_____
_____
_____
_____

Pyramid of Importance: Each character in the story holds a position of importance. Some are of main importance, some are of less importance. Student will fill in the pyramid with the names of the characters. The top should have the most important character, the next line the next most important characters and continue down until you have listed all the characters in order of importance.

Poetry Form: Student will write a poem about the book or characters using this format.

Lantern: A lantern is a five line poem in the shape of a Japanese lantern. The Pattern is:
Line 1: noun (one syllable)
Line 2: describe the noun (two syllables)
Line 3: describe the noun (three syllables
Line 4: describe the noun (four syllables)
Line 5: Synonym for noun in line one (one syllable)

Example:	Mane
	long, thick
	blonde to black
	royal mantle
	Fur

Newspaper Activity: Student will use this form to write their newspaper piece on then paste it onto their newspaper lay out poster.

Entertainment Section: Book Review Student will write an over all review of the book and tell what they liked and did not like, which characters seemed real and which scenes were described the best. Student should also ad a picture of the book cover.

Book Review

Creative Writing Activity:
Newberry Award: Each year one book is chosen to receive the John Newberry Award for great writing. Student will write a short report on why this book did or should have won the award.

Writing Skills Activity: Student will use this form or write in their notebook.

Climax: The climax of a story is the point where the reader knows who wins the conflict or how the problem will be solved. Student will write what the main problem was and at what point they knew how it would be solved.

Lapbook Activity: **Mini Book:** Student will make a mini book about this story or about a subject in the story. See the pattern on one of the following pages.

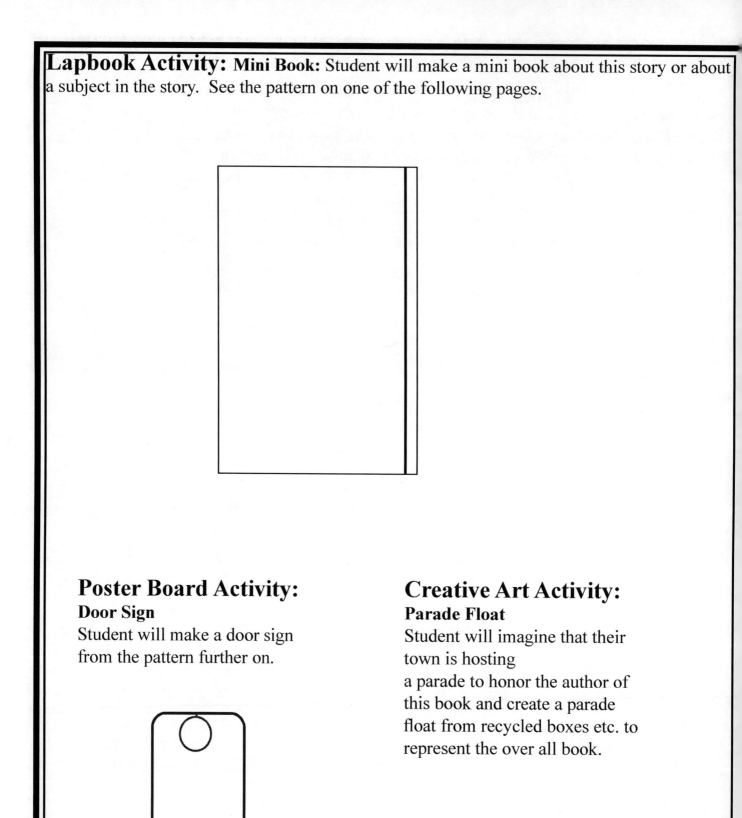

Poster Board Activity:
Door Sign
Student will make a door sign from the pattern further on.

Creative Art Activity:
Parade Float
Student will imagine that their town is hosting
a parade to honor the author of this book and create a parade float from recycled boxes etc. to represent the over all book.

Door Sign: On a piece of poster board student will create a sign for their bedroom door that represents something from the book.

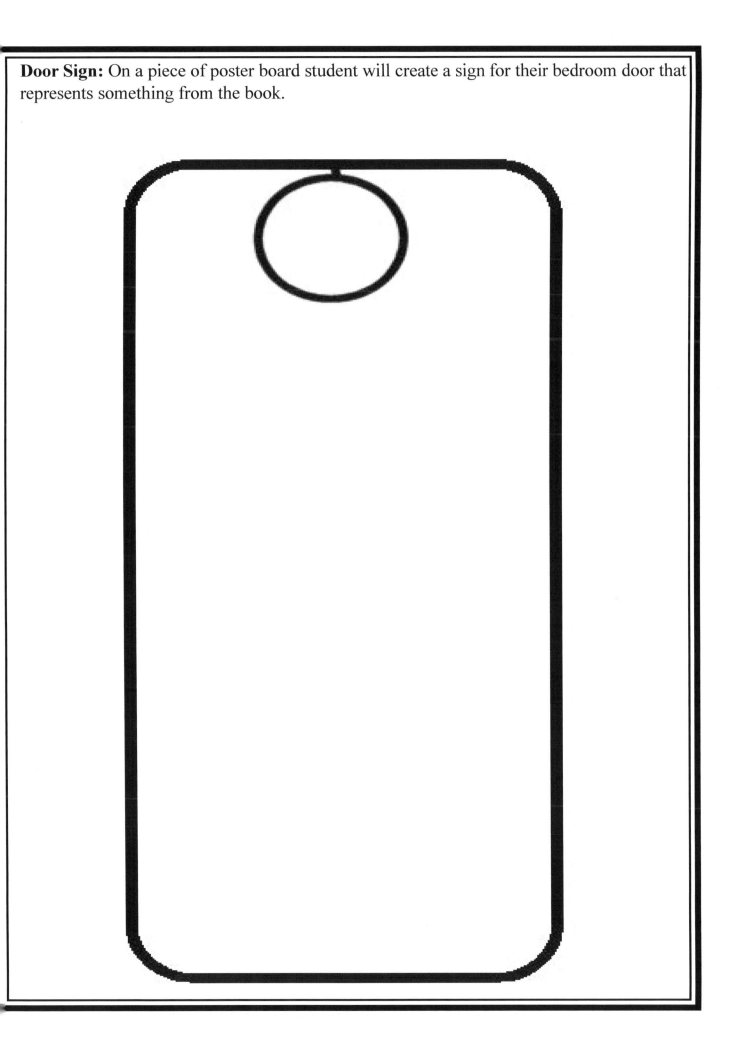

Mini Book : Student will create a mini book that retells the story. This may be put on the Lapbook.

12   1

2　　　　　　　　　　　　　　　　　　　　　11

Print double sided. Cut on the red lines. Fold on the dotted lines.

10 3

8 5

Print double sided. Cut on the red lines. Fold on the dotted lines.

4

9

6

7

Lesson 10 Activities

Lesson 10 Activities: Students will use the book they are studying and information found on the internet for the following activities. Then the student will write the information required for this activity on the patterns or in their notebook. The patterns may be cut out and placed on the lapbook.

Encyclopedia:
Student will choose one subject from this lesson that interested them and look it up on the internet or in encyclopedia. They will write the name of the subject across the top of the monitor pattern. On the monitor screen section, they will write three or more interesting facts about the subject.

Journal:
Student will imagine that they are one of the characters from the story. After reading each lesson, they will write a short journal entry telling what happened from that character's point of view.
Student will also draw a picture to go along with the journal entry.
At the end of the book, student will staple all the journal entries together to form a complete booklet.
They can even create a special cover for it from construction paper.

Vocabulary word: _____
Definition of the word: _____
_____
_____

Antonym of the word: _____
How many syllables does the word have? _____

Vocabulary Word: _____
Sentence using the word: _____
_____
_____

Synonym of the word: _____

Vocabulary: Student will use the vocabulary words from the list for this lesson. On one of the patterns, or on one index card they will write one vocabulary word. They should also write the definition of the word, then the Antonym and how many Syllables the word has.

On the other card, the student will write the same word. They will write a full sentence using this word and then write the Synonym of the word.

They will repeat this for all the vocabulary words in this lesson.

Place the patterns or cards in an envelope which can be glued into the student's notebook or onto the lapbook..

Sequencing: At the end of the lesson the student will write two of the main events on these two strips. Save them in an envelope which can be glued onto the lapbook or in the notebook. At the end of the book, these strips can be taken out and the student can arrange them in the correct order as they occurred in the story.

Handwriting: Student will pick their favorite sentence that they read in this lesson. Have them write the sentence in their best handwriting on this page or in their notebook.

Student will write out the answers for the following:
Main Idea: In a sentence or two, write what the main idea was of this section.

_____
_____
_____
_____
_____

Key Event: In a sentence or two write what the most important event was in this section.

_____
_____
_____
_____
_____
_____
_____

Prediction: In a sentence of two write what you Predict will happen in the next section.

_____
_____
_____
_____
_____
_____
_____

Comparison: In a sentence of two compare two things in this section. Tell what makes them alike and what makes them different.

_____
_____
_____
_____
_____
_____

Fact or Opinion: In one sentence write a fact about this section and one sentence that is an opinion about the lesson.

_____
_____
_____
_____
_____
_____

Hero vs. Villain: Most stories usually have a hero (the main character) and a villain. The villain may not seem that bad. The villain is usually the character who stands in the way of the main character, or against the main character. Student will name the Hero and the Villain and fill in the "What the Villain does...." square.

Hero

What the Villain does to hinder the Hero.

Villain

Poetry Form: Student will write a poem about the book or characters using this format.

Shape Poem: To be done on a separate sheet of paper. Shape poems can be made by placing words, which describe a particular object, in such a way that they form the shape of the object. Student will start by making a simple outline of the shape or object (an animal, a football, a fruit etc.) large enough to fill a piece of paper. Then student will brainstorm a minimum of ten words and phrases that describe the shape including action and feeling words as well. Next, student will place a piece of paper over the shape and decide where the words are going to be placed so that they outline the shape but also fit well together. Separate words and phrases with commas. Shape poems can also be created by simply filling in the shape with a poem, as well.

Newspaper Activity: Student will use this form to write their newspaper piece on then paste it onto their newspaper lay out poster.

Word Search Section: Find all the words

```
G D P S Z D E T A D I M I T N I N E E F
E N I R H E E M A L I C I O U S O L A P
H S I S O A L T C U R E I L C A I B V R
T T O T T M M B A E M T O E U I S A E E
Y N B U N I I E A N A E Y S R M N T S T
C E P N D I N S F R O M P S D P E C D E
S M U C R R O G E A E I E O L U C E R R
U T N H U H A P U H C L N N E L S P O N
O N C A O B S G P I B E O I D S E S P A
R A T S G A C S O A S X D T P E D E P T
E H I T X X A U N O S H Y L N O N R E U
P C L E K L S I I N N I E N Y I O E D R
E N I N B L A I N E M S D D P D C S E A
R E O E Y L C O N S T E R N A T I O N L
T G U D P D E Z I L A D N A C S T L I O
S G S X H T L A E W N O M M O C E U R Y
B Y E L B I T S I S E R R I T O R T G A
O N I N D I F F E R E N C E T W E I A L
U C O N S E Q U E N C E S X Q L H O H T
R E A L I Z A T I O N W B U O Y A N C Y
```

AUSPICIOUSLY	BLASPHEMY	BUOYANCY	CHAGRINED
COMMONWEALTH	CONDESCENSION	CONSEQUENCES	CONSTERNATION
CURDLED	CURE	DISAPPOINTING	DISTINGUISHED
DRAGOONS	EAVESDROPPED	ENCHANTMENTS	EXASPERATION
GOURD	HERETIC	IMPULSE	INDIFFERENCE
INTIMIDATED	INTOLERABLE	IRRESISTIBLE	LESSON
LOYALTY	MALICIOUS	MENIAL	OBSTREPEROUS
OPINIONATED	PRETERNATURAL	PROMISE	PUNCTILIOUS
REALIZATION	RESOLUTION	RESPECTABLE	SCANDALIZED
SCOWL	SCYTHE	SHAMEFACEDLY	UNCHASTENED
UNEXPLAINABLE			

Creative Writing Activity: A Different End: Student will write a different ending for the story.

Writing Skills Activity: Plot Analysis Board

Student will create this by following the directions.

What you need:
Index Cards, Pictures from the internet, Markers, Crayons. Glue

1. Fold the poster board in half so that it makes a folder.
2. Decorate the front of the folder with pictures and information that includes the Title, the Author, the Illustrator, and the Publisher.
3. On index cards, write the information requested below. Glue the index cards inside the folder. You can put pictures on the cards to go along with them.

   Information to put on cards:
   1. Main Character and Character Traits
   2. Main Setting
   3. Other Characters
   4. Other Settings in the Story
   5. Main Problem
   6. Other Problems
   7. Climax
   8. Solution to the Problem
   9. Your favorite part of the story
   10. What you would change if you could about the story.

Lapbook Activity: The Commandments: Student will cut out the patter and fold so that the Ten Commandments are on the front. Inside student will write how a character may have broken or upheld one or more of these commandments. Attach to Lapbook.

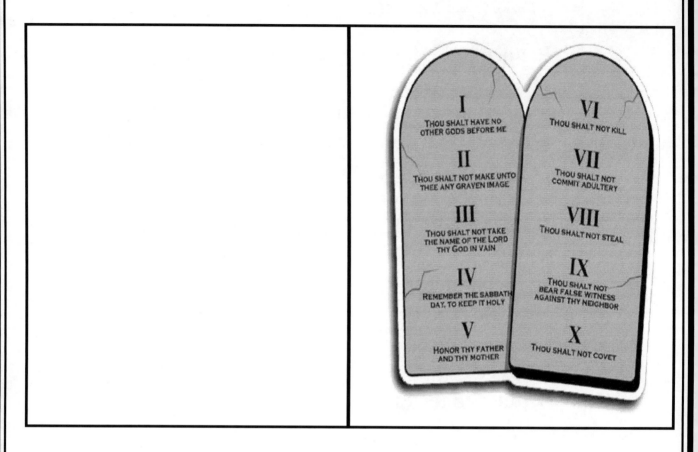

Poster Board Activity:
Jeopardy
On the poster board student will create a game board like the one on the next page. They will cut out several sets of the play money. The teacher will write 4 to 8 questions for each category. The student then picks one category and the dollar amount of the question they will try and answer. The teacher or student reads the question. If the answer is correct the student wins the amount of money that they chose. The next player takes a turn. The winner is the one with the most

Creative Art Activity:
Sketch
Student will imagine they are a sketch artist and using black pencils or charcoal pencils, they will sketch some of the main characters, places or events from the story.

JEOPARDY

People	Places	Animals	Other
$100	$100	$100	$100
$200	$200	$200	$200
$300	$300	$300	$300
$400	$400	$400	$400

Additional Activities

Additional Writing Activities

Imaginative: Imaginative writing is when you write a fanciful story using your imagination. Student will write one that comes to mind while they read this book.

Essay: An essay is a short piece of writing, from an author's personal point of view. Student will write a short essay from their point of view about a subject that comes to mind while reading these books.

Speech: A speech is the act of delivering a formal spoken communication to an audience . Student will write a short speech that one of the characters from the books may have given.

Autobiography: An autobiography is a story of a person's life. Student will write a short autobiography outline of one of the characters or they could write about the author as well.

Humor: Humor allows the reader to laugh and enjoy a story. Student will write a humorous piece about a subject or thing mentioned in these books.

ABC Story: ABC Stories are short stories that have each sentence starting with the next letter in the alphabet. Student will write a short ABC story about an event or one of the characters in the book. For example:
 A girl named Kit lived in America. By noon she was happy...

Literature Web: A story will make you think of many things and feel many things. Student will draw this chart in their notebook and fill it in.

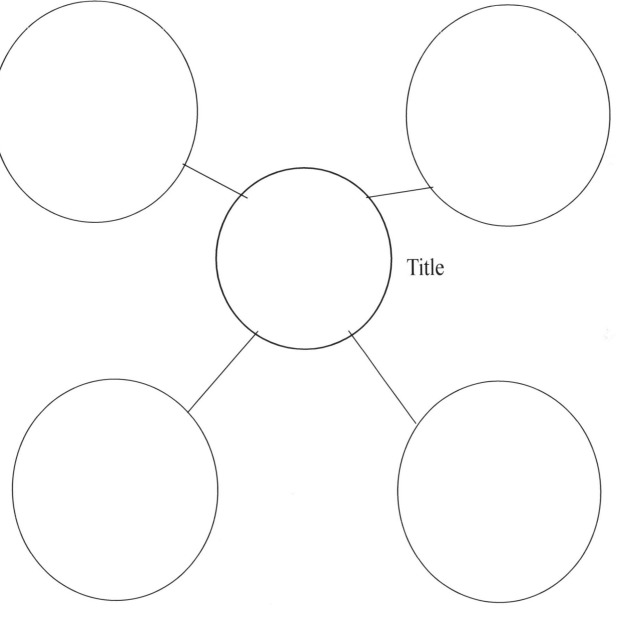

Key Words: What were some important words or phrases?

Feelings: What feelings did you have while reading the book?

Title

Symbols: Did the author use any symbols in the story?

Attitude: What do you think the authors attitude is about the subject this story is about?

Sign Language:

On a piece of poster board, student will glue a larger versions of the sign language alphabet. Now the teacher will sign a name, scene or vocabulary word from the story. Students try to figure the word out by pointing to the correct sign language letter and spelling out the words.

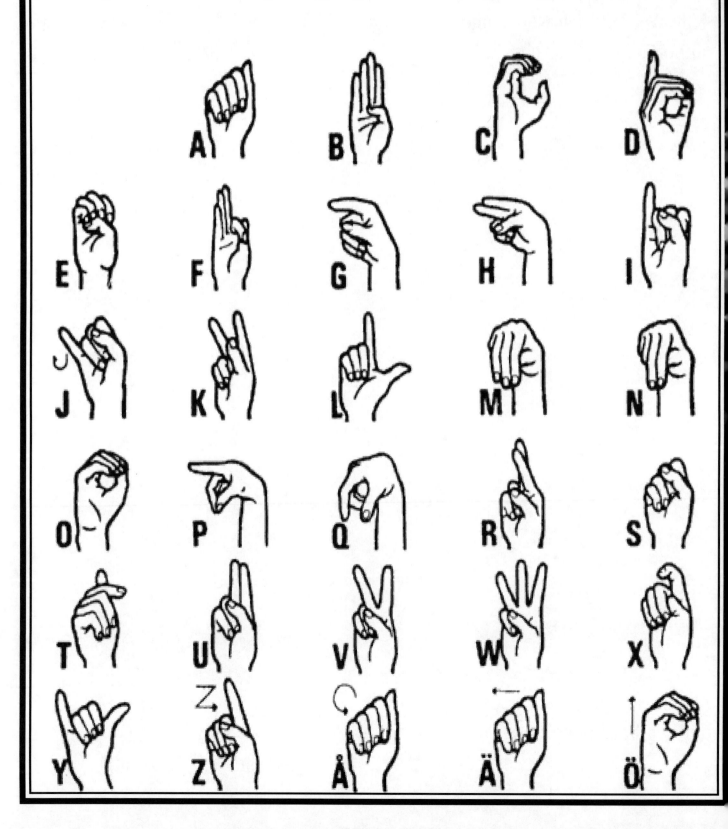

Theater Box:

Get a cardboard box with a flat side larger than a piece of paper. In the side cut out a square about 6 by 9 inches. This will be the opening for your theater.

While reading each chapter of the book, Student will draw one or more of the main scenes on 8 1/2 by 11 inch drawing paper. Stay within the inner 6 by 9 inches though. Color these with markers, paint, colored pencils etc.

Figure out a way that these pictures can be slid in and out of the box, so they appear in the opening and it looks like you are changing scenes, or draw them all on one long roll, and create rollers in each end of the box out of paper towel rolls.

At the end of the book you should have a whole story in these scenes. Present the scenes in your theater to family or friends. You will have to act as the announcer and explain the main events in each scene.

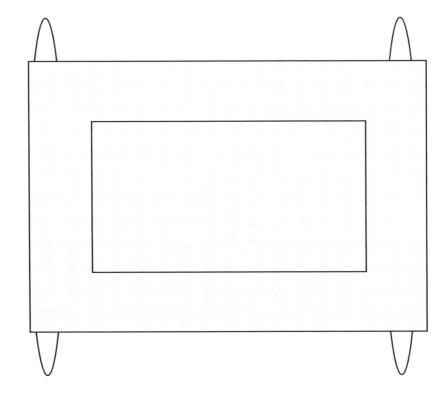

Acting: Student will

1. Dress up as one of the characters in the story. They can act out their favorite part of the story.
2. Host a talk show where another member of the family acts as the television host. Your student is the main character of the story. They ask you questions about the story.
3. Hold a trial. Someone dresses up as the villain in the story. Someone dresses up as the main character. Someone as a lawyer and someone as a judge. Hold a trial to determine if the villain is really guilty of crimes or not.

Rock Art:
Student will gather smooth rocks of different shapes and sizes. Student will clean the rocks and when dry create characters from the book with the rocks, by painting them, making clothes for them and gluing on google eyes.

Name Art:
Student will write the main characters name in the middle of 1/4 poster board and then decorate all around it in any art form they like.

Carving:

Use soap or wax and carve a character from the story. All you need to carve soap is a bar of soap and a spoon. If your child is old enough to use a butter knife then you can let them have a butter knife to carve their soap with. Soap carving can be messy so it is best to be done on a table covered with an old cloth or newspaper. And everyone doing the carving should have old clothes on.

When carving soap, you can use any size bar of soap you would like, but a nice big bar of soap is better to get creative with. If you are lucky enough to have a bar of home made lye soap that will work as well. Unwrap your bar of soap and decide what you want to make with your bar of soap. Soap is a soft material so a spoon will work to carve a bar of soap just fine. A knife can give your bar of soap more detail then a spoon can but it is more dangerous.

Sewing:

Use felt and material stuffing. Create a pattern for something from the story such as an animal or character. Cut out two of the same patterns from the felt. Have student sew around the outside edges. Stuff with stuffing and complete the sewing.

Design a Needlepoint:
Get graph paper and have student design a needlepoint by placing an x in the boxes to design the picture.

Shape Puzzle: On poster board student will draw out a large copy of the shape of a character or item from the book. Cut it into a puzzle pattern.

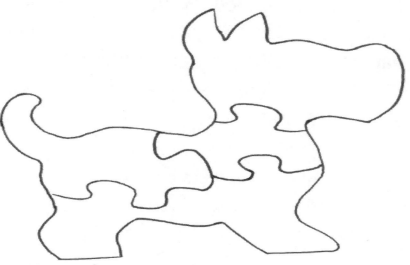

I Spy

Student will find pictures on the internet of things that come to mind while reading this book. Pictures of the characters, of the vocabulary words etc. Student will print and then glue them all over the poster board. Now they should make an I spy set of calling cards on index cards.

For example your cards would say:

I spy a cat.

I spy a rat.

Give the cards to a younger child and see if they can find all the items on the I spy poster.

Bingo: Print as many of these Bingo boards as you need for the students. Write the vocabulary words in the squares of the Bingo boards. Each board should be different. Use the definition index cards as the call cards for the game.

B	I	N	G	O
		Free Space		

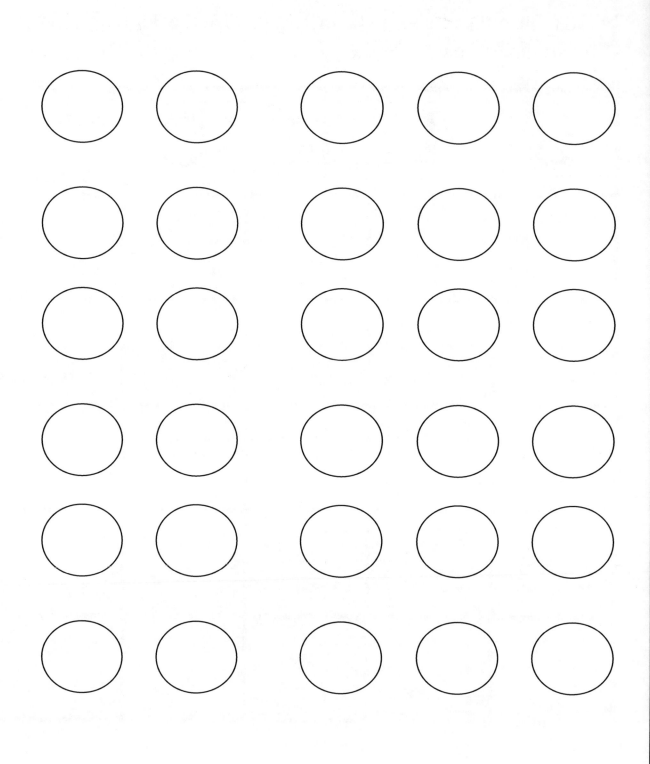

Comprehension

The following pages have the
Fill in the Blanks,
True and False,
Multiple Choice
and
Who, What, Where, When,
Why and How Questions
for all lessons.

Use the Vocabulary words
on the following page for the
questions

Lesson 1	Chapter 1,2
Lesson 2	Chapter 3,4
Lesson 3	Chapter 5,6,7
Lesson 4	Chapter 8,9
Lesson 5	Chapter 10,11
Lesson 6	Chapter 12,13
Lesson 7	Chapter 14,15
Lesson 8	Chapter 16,17
Lesson 9	Chapter 18,19
Lesson 10	Chapter 20,21

Here are the Assigned Chapters and Vocabulary Words for each lesson.

Lesson 1. brigantine   disappointing   shrew   contrast   impulse   becalmed punctilious   scandalized   curdled   pinnaces

Lesson 2. chagrined   respectable   scowl   realization   pondering   gruel   indigo gaudy   intimidated   advantage

Lesson 3. frippery   auspiciously   pillory   reverent   duplicate   allegiance condescension   opinionated   hypocrite   irresistible

Lesson 4. menial   calico   prickled   primer   finicky   obstreperous   bedlam   cure gourd   unexplainable

Lesson 5. promise   malicious   branded   Quakers   sacraments   exasperation filigree   unfailing   consequences   deceiving

Lesson 6. shamefacedly   mockery   scythe   loyalty   consternation   heretic contagious   predict   propitious   foreboding

Lesson 7. buoyancy   eavesdropped   distraction   paupers   commonwealth distinguished   grenadiers   cavalier   dragoons   militia

Lesson 8. unchastened   roistering   blasphemy   treatise   premonition   poultice resolution   exhausted   bounden   wraithlike

Lesson 9. conscience   gainsay   sustained   evidence   inveigled   respectable   cronies preternatural   countenance   enchantments

Lesson 10. curious   bygones   judged   levelly   intolerable   intentions   dowries indifference   governess   ketch

Lesson 1   Chapter 1,2

Fill in the Blanks: Write the vocabulary word that best completes the sentence.
Words: contrast   disappointing   shrew   becalmed   punctilious

1. As Kit examined her first glimpse of America she had found it very _____.
2. The shoreline was a big _____ from the beautiful green and white bay of Barbados.
3. The other passengers considered the _____ ship a bad sign that Kit brought about.
4. The Goodwife Cruff was a very _____ of a mother toward her little girl.
5. Captain Eaton treated Kit with _____ caution.

True / False: Write T if statement is true; write F if it is false.

1. _____ The Dolphin was badly damaged during the storm at sea.
2. _____ There was only two women on the voyage, Kit and the Captain's wife.
3. _____ Kit's grandfather taught her how to swim as soon as she could walk.
4. _____ The trip to Wethersfield was a quick-run for the Dolphin it only took a few days to get there.

Multiple Choice: Write ABCD in the space for the best answer.

1. _____ Nathaniel Eaton is _____ of the Dolphin.
A. the first mate
B. the captain's son
C. a passenger on the Dolphin
D. both A and B

2. _____ The Port of Saybrook is home to _____.
A. Kit's uncle
B. the Eatons
C. Kit's grandfather
D. Kit's aunt

3. _____ Who is Kit going to live with?
A. her aunt and uncle Matthew Wood
B. The Eatons
C. the Reverend Bulkeley and his wife
D. The Mayor of Wethersfield and his wife

4. _____ Who did Kit's aunt marry?
A. a soldier
B. a sailor
C. a teacher
D. a Puritan

Lesson 1
Write full sentences for this section:

1. Who is Kit's grandfather?
2. What is the water trial?
3. Where was Kit born?
4. When Captain Eaton takes a job what is the one thing he will not haul?
5. Why did Captain Eaton have to use a device called "walking up the river"?
6. How did Kit learn to keep her balance on the ship?

(Who) _____
_____
_____
_____

(What) _____
_____
_____
_____

(Where) _____
_____
_____
_____

(When) _____
_____
_____
_____

(Why) _____
_____
_____
_____

(How) _____
_____
_____
_____

Lesson 2   Chapter 3,4

Fill in the Blanks: Write the vocabulary word that best completes the sentence.
Words: respectable   gaudy   scowl   intimidated   realization

1. Matthew Wood's house looked solid and _____ compared to the cabins Kit had passed.
2. Suddenly Kit's _____ of the past four months swept over her as she saw her aunt approach.
3. Kit was aware that not a motion had escaped Matthew's intended _____.
4. Judith was not _____, she bravely faced her father telling him Kit had given her the dress.
5. Matthew allowed Mercy to keep the blue scarf because it was not _____.

True / False: Write T if statement is true; write F if it is false.

1. _____ Kit was so excited to find the town of Wethersfield was quite large and promising.
2. _____ Kit's uncle will not allow her to stay in his house for more than a few months.
3. _____ Matthew will not allow anyone of his household to ware any of Kit's clothes.
4. _____ The one weakness of Matthew was his love for his daughter Mercy.

Multiple Choice: Write ABCD in the space for the best answer.

1. _____ What did Matthew allow Mercy to keep?
A. lace gloves
B. a light blue wool shawl
C. a hat
D. a dress

2. _____ Why did Kit leave Barbados?
A. a fifty year old rich man wanted to marry her
B. she wanted a new adventure
C. she wanted to see America
D. she wanted to go to college

3. _____ What qualities did Kit seem not to have?
A. skill
B. patience
C. anger
D. both A and B

4. _____ What was one of the ingredients that homemade soap has?
A. onion
B. garlic
C. lye
D. sugar

Lesson 2
Write full sentences for this section:

1. Who is Rachel, Judith and Mercy?
2. What rule did Matthew set before Kit?
3. Where was Kit to sleep?
4. When Kit's grandfather was robbed of his crop money what happened?
5. Why didn't Kit send a letter asking her aunt and uncle if she could live with them?
6. How do you make corn pudding?

(Who) _____

(What) _____

(Where) _____

(When) _____

(Why) _____

(How) _____

Lesson 3   Chapter 5,6,7

Fill in the Blanks: Write the vocabulary word that best completes the sentence.
Words: irresistible   pillory   allegiance   reverent   duplicate

1. Kit was shocked by the objects that stood between her and the church; a _____, whipping post, and stocks.
2. All of the church goers were alike in their _____ silence.
3. There's not a cook in the colonies who can _____ Rachel's apple tarts.
4. Reverend Bulkeley was questioning Kit's _____ to King James.
5. There is something _____ about popcorn.

True / False: Write T if statement is true; write F if it is false.

1. _____ In the meeting house the men sat on one side and the women sat on the other.
2. _____ The Sabbath house and small lean-to is where church members cook and stay warm.
3. _____ In Connecticut the people don't like the new governor that King James put in power.
4. _____ William Ashby is interested in courting Judith.

Multiple Choice: Write ABCD in the space for the best answer.

1. _____ What did Kit wear to church?
A. her flowered silk dress
B. a plain blue and white dress the same as her Aunt Rachel's
C. a black dress
D. a blue checkered dress

2. _____ What distraction took place at the church service?
A. a baby had the hiccups
B. one little girl sneezed
C. one of the young boys caught a fly and hid it
D. a cat was chasing a mouse

3. _____ What favorite snack did Aunt Rachel offer the group?
A. bananas
B. pop-corn
C. cookies
D. tarts

4. _____ What did the King's charter guarantee?
A. rights and laws
B. privileges
C. land
D. all the above

Lesson 3
Write full sentences for this section:

1. Who was knighted for his loyalty by King Charles?
2. What did the town assembly vote on?
3. Where is William going to build his house?
4. When was the people of Connecticut given a charter from King Charles?
5. Why does the assembly want all the land claimed?
6. How many church services do the Puritans have on the Sabbath?

(Who) _____

(What) _____

(Where) _____

(When) _____

(Why) _____

(How) _____

Lesson 4   Chapter 8,9

Fill in the Blanks: Write the vocabulary word that best completes the sentence.
Words: prickled   primer   cure   obstreperous   menial

1. The dress Rachel and Mercy made Kit was more suited for _____ work.
2. When Kit looked back at the little house in the meadows her spine _____.
3. Kit was in charge of the _____ readers and Mercy was teaching the beginners.
4. The mistake made was to chose three _____ pupils to be thieves and robbers.
5. Hannah told Kit that there is always a _____ in the meadows when the heart is troubled.

True / False: Write T if statement is true; write F if it is false.

1. _____ In the Great Meadows where nobody lives Kit saw a little cottage.
2. _____ Widow Tupper is loved by everyone in Wethersfield and the Meeting House.
3. _____ Mr. Kimberley thought that Kit's methods of teaching were new and exciting.
4. _____ Hannah had a flower bulb that came from the Cape of Good Hope, from Africa.

Multiple Choice: Write ABCD in the space for the best answer.

1. _____ In the Great Meadows what reminded Kit of home?
A. freedom
B. space
C. light
D. all the above

2. _____ What promise did the meadows hold for Kit?
A. peace
B. comfort
C. quietness
D. all the above

3. _____ What did the children use in place of paper?
A. wax tablets
B. birch bark
C. corn husks
D. deer skins

4. _____ How many students were in the school?
A. eight boys
B. three girls
C. eleven in all
D. all the above

Lesson 4
Write full sentences for this section:

1. Who runs a summer school for the young children?
2. What is a hornbook?
3. Where does Hannah Tupper live?
4. When Kit had only the Bible to read to the children what stories did she choose?
5. Why did Rachel and Mercy make a calico dress for Kit?
6. How important is the Dame School in Wethersfield?

(Who) _____

(What) _____

(Where) _____

(When) _____

(Why) _____

(How) _____

Lesson 5   Chapter 10,11

Fill in the Blanks: Write the vocabulary word that best completes the sentence.
Words: malicious   filigree   Quakers   unfailing   branded

1. Rachel said that calling Hannah Tupper a witch was just _____ gossip.
2. _____ are queer stubborn people who don't believe in the Sacraments.
3. Hannah and her husband were _____ and driven out of Massachusetts because they were Quakers.
4. The little hornbook was backed by silver _____ and underlaid with red satin.
5. Love was the invisible ingredient that made Hannah's cures _____.

True / False: Write T if statement is true; write F if it is false.

1. _____ Mr. Kimberley is not a man known for changing his mind.
2. _____ Aunt Rachel did not see any harm in Kit visiting Hannah.
3. _____ Mr. Kimberley told Mercy and Kit to smile at the children at school.
4. _____ Prudence can not go to school because her mother says she's stupid.

Multiple Choice: Write ABCD in the space for the best answer.

1. _____ What kind of a person is Hannah Tupper?
A. gentle
B. kind
C. good
D. all the above

2. _____ In what secret place did Kit find freedom, peace, and sunlight?
A. the local church
B. the meadow
C. the meeting house
D. the seashore

3. _____ Who is Hannah's seafaring friend?
A. Captain Blood
B. Captain Blackbeard
C. Nathaniel Eaton
D. Captain Jones

4. _____ Who has been leaving flowers at the school for Kit?
A. Prudence
B. John
C. William
D. Nathaniel

Lesson 5
Write full sentences for this section:

1. Who changed his mind and gave Kit another chance?
2. What is Hannah's cure for every illness?
3. Where did Kit find a hornbook for Prudence?
4. When John was reading for the Woods family what did Kit notice?
5. Why do most folks in Wethersfield not like Hannah?
6. How does Mr. Kimberley feel about children?

(Who) _____
_____
_____

(What) _____
_____
_____
_____

(Where) _____
_____
_____
_____

(When) _____
_____
_____
_____

(Why) _____
_____
_____
_____

(How) _____
_____
_____
_____

Lesson 6   Chapter 12,13

Fill in the Blanks: Write the vocabulary word that best completes the sentence.
Words: mockery   loyalty   scythe   foreboding   contagious

1. Today Kit was in the mood to overlook Nat's _____ of her.
2. Kit gathered the long grasses that Nat had fell with his _____.
3. Nat believes there are two sides to _____.
4. Judith's excitement was so _____ that Kit began to feel a tingle of excitement herself.
5. Judith's teasing always seemed to raise a little cold lump of _____ in Kit's throat.

True / False: Write T if statement is true; write F if it is false.

1. _____ Aunt Rachel can't bear to think of anyone going hungry when others have plenty.
2. _____ Nat believes that if the king respects the people's rights and keeps his word they will retain their loyalty.
3. _____ John was very happy to hear that Kit has been helping Hannah.
4. _____ Mercy doesn't have Judith's pride; it was something stronger than pride that upheld her.

Multiple Choice: Write ABCD in the space for the best answer.

1. _____ What did Rachel make cider from?
A. wild pears
B. strawberries
C. blueberries
D. crab apples

2. _____ What thing does Nat and Kit have in common?
A. they love the sea
B. higher education
C. they love books
D. apple tarts

3. _____ In Kit's day what was a cure for asthma?
A. spinach
B. skunk cabbage
C. apples
D. mustard greens

4. _____ Who found the first bright-red ear of corn?
A. John
B. William
C. Mercy
D. Judith

Lesson 6

Write full sentences for this section:

1. Who is in love with Mercy?
2. What was the first party that Kit had ever been invited to in Wethersfield?
3. Where is a man's first loyalty?
4. When John arrived at the Wood's home what was his intentions?
5. Why did John agree to marry Judith?
6. How did the Woods family make candles?

(Who) _____

_____

_____

_____

(What) _____

_____

_____

_____

(Where) _____

_____

_____

_____

(When) _____

_____

_____

_____

(Why) _____

_____

_____

_____

(How) _____

_____

_____

_____

Lesson 7   Chapter 14,15

Fill in the Blanks: Write the vocabulary word that best completes the sentence.
Words: buoyancy   commonwealths   distraction   cavalier   dragoons

1. Every morning Kit awakened with a new confidence and _____ she could not explain.
2. When Kit and Judith reached home a _____ awaited them.
3. If Governor Andros takes over Connecticut it means the death of the free _____.
4. Governor Andros used to be a captain of the _____ in Barbados.
5. Andros was a true _____ in his fine coat, commanding air, and dark curls.

True / False: Write T if statement is true; write F if it is false.

1. _____ Kit gazed with wonder as she discovered the breathless autumn in New England.
2. _____ If Andros takes over, the people of Connecticut will have to beg for new land grants they have already paid for.
3. _____ Dr. Bulkeley felt that the charter is a fair guarantee for the people of Connecticut.
4. _____ Everyone in New England celebrates All Hallows Eve.

Multiple Choice: Write ABCD in the space for the best answer.

1. _____ What did the Dolphin deliver for William Ashby's house?
A. two doors
B. paint
C. sixteen windows
D. large nails

2. _____ Why is William building a house?
A. for his bride
B. to sell later for a good price
C. his parent's house is to small
D. he wants to rent it

3. _____ How many trained men are ready to fight in Hartford?
A. 100
B. 250
C. 500
D. 1,000

4. _____ Whom did Judith think might know where the charter is?
A. Governor Treat
B. Dr. Bulkeley
C. William
D. John

Lesson 7
Write full sentences for this section:

1. Who was a member of the militia in Hartford?
2. What happened to the charter?
3. Where was the charter before it disappeared?
4. When did the rider alert the people of Wethersfield about the change in governors?
5. Why did Nat want Kit to go to Hannahs?
6. How does Uncle Matthew feel about his land?

(Who) _____

(What) _____

(Where) _____

(When) _____

(Why) _____

(How) _____

Lesson 8   Chapter 16,17

Fill in the Blanks: Write the vocabulary word that best completes the sentence.
Words: poultice   roistering   premonition   exhausted   resolution

1. On All Hallows Eve three sailors came _____ into town and pulled a prank on William.
2. Kit had a _____ that this may be the last day she will see Hannah and Prudence.
3. Dr. Bulkeley placed a _____ of hot onions on Mercy's chest so she could breath better.
4. Hannah's _____ gave way and all at once she and Kit ran for their lives.
5. Hannah was _____ all her strength had died with the dying flames of her home.

True / False: Write T if statement is true; write F if it is false.

1. _____ The new governor declared there would be no Thanksgiving holiday this week.
2. _____ All three sailors in the stock did not belong to the Dolphin.
3. _____ Kit admitted that she is in love with William Ashby.
4. _____ There is a mysterious fever going around the town and the Woods have come down with it.

Multiple Choice: Write ABCD in the space for the best answer

1. _____ What is Thursdays Lecture Day?
A. the day the judge visits the town
B. the day of public punishment
C. the day of the school spelling bee
D. the day of the schools essay contest

2. _____ What sentence did Nat and his two friends receive for their prank?
A. sit in the stocks one hour before the Lecture
B. sit in the stocks one hour after the Lecture
C. they are forbidden to enter the boundary's of Wethersfield
D. all the above

3. _____ What did Kit give Prudence?
A. a bottle of ink
B. a copybook
C. a quill pen
D. all the above

4. _____ Who came to help Mercy?
A. Dr. Bulkeley
B. Hanna
C. John
D. Nat

Lesson 8
Write full sentences for this section:

1. Who's house seemed to look much less desperate to Kit?
2. What happened on All Hollows Eve?
3. Where is John going?
4. When a mob came to the Wood's house what did they want?
5. Why will there be no Thanksgiving holiday in Wethersfield this year?
6. How did Kit describe the change in Prudence?

(Who) _____

(What) _____

(Where) _____

(When) _____

(Why) _____

(How) _____

Lesson 9   Chapter 18,19

Fill in the Blanks: Write the vocabulary word that best completes the sentence.
Words: sustained   enchantments   respectable   conscience   countenance

1. Kit wished she never deceived her uncle and wanted to stand before him with a clear _____.
2. Kit, _____ by her aunt's visit was able to face the morning without panic.
3. Washing her face and combing her hair Kit felt more _____.
4. Captain Talcott had a distaste for the duty ahead, but his soldierly _____ did not soften.
5. Kit was accused of using _____ with the intent of causing mischief to people.

True / False: Write T if statement is true; write F if it is false.

1. _____ Goodwife Cruff accused Hanna of changing herself into a great fat mouse.
2. _____ The constable has charged Kit with witchcraft.
3. _____ Reverend Woodbridge and Dr. Bulkeley are famous for their sermons on witchcraft.
4. _____ William was at the trial ready to speak in behalf of Kit's innocence.

Multiple Choice: Write ABCD in the space for the best answer.

1. _____ Kit felt better because _____.
A. Hanna was safe
B. Mercy was getting well
C. the harvest was over
D. both A and B

2. _____ What did the mob find at Hanna's house?
A. Kit's silver hornbook
B. Kit's cap
C. Kit's necklace
D. Kit's ring

3. _____ Who is the magistrate from the General Court of Connecticut?
A. Edmond Andros
B. Captain Samuel Talcott
C. Captain Cruff
D. Dr. Bulkeley

4. _____ What is Kit being accused of?
A. being a friend of Widow Tupper, a supposed witch
B. guilty of actions which caused illness and death to the town
C. both A and B
D. being disobedient

Lesson 9
Write full sentences for this section:

1. Who came to the Wood's house the next morning after Hanna escaped?
2. What was found in Hanna's house that may have proved Kit a witch?
3. Where did the constable lock Kit up for the night?
4. When the trial was over what did Prudence's father ask her to do?
5. Why did Nat bring Prudence to the trial?
6. How had Prudence been treated by her mother?

(Who) _____

(What) _____

(Where) _____

(When) _____

(Why) _____

(How) _____

Lesson 10   Chapter 20,21

Fill in the Blanks: Write the vocabulary word that best completes the sentence.
Words: judged   bygones   intentions   curious   governess

1. The snow was _____ and lovely in its own way, but it makes everything so dark.
2. William told Kit that when she goes back to town everyone is glad to let _____ be _____.
3. William believes that people are _____ by the company they keep.
4. On a Lecture Day in April two marriage _____ were announced in the Meeting House.
5. Kit believed that she could find employment as a _____ with a wealthy family.

True / False: Write T if statement is true; write F if it is false.

1. _____ This is the first time Kit had ever seen snow.
2. _____ Kit was in awe of the lovely blue sky and the beauty of the white world around her.
3. _____ All the men from Wethersfield were ambushed by the Indians and none had survived.
4. _____ All the Puritans in town celebrated Christmas with great rejoicing.

Multiple Choice: Write ABCD in the space for the best answer.

1. _____ What does Mercy love better than anything in the world?
A. the sea
B. the first snowfall
C. the spring rains
D. the hot summer days

2. _____ Who was one of the militia that fell captive to the Indians?
A. John Holbrook
B. Dr. Bulkeley
C. Natheniel
D. Captain Alcott

3. _____ Who did Judith marry?
A. John
B. Nat
C. William
D. Captain Alcott's son

4. _____ Who did Mercy marry?
A. William
B. Nat
C. Tom
D. John

Lesson 10
Write full sentences for this section:

1. Who did Kit realize she really loved?
2. What surprise did Kit have as she waited on the wharf?
3. Where did Kit want to be?
4. When is the double wedding taking place?
5. Why did William and Kit end their engagement?
6. How many different kinds of cake were at Thankful's wedding?

(Who) _____
_____
_____
_____

(What) _____
_____
_____
_____

(Where) _____
_____
_____
_____

(When) _____
_____
_____
_____

(Why) _____
_____
_____
_____

(How) _____
_____
_____
_____

Answer Key

Lesson 1
Fill in the Blanks
1. disappointing
2. contrast
3. becalmed
4. shrew
5. punctilious
True and False
1. F
2. T
3. T
4. F
Multiple Choice
1. D
2. B
3. A
4. D
Who, What, Where, When, Why, and How
1. Sir Francis Tyler
2. a witch will float in the water; the innocent just sink like stone
3. Barbados in the West Indies
4. slaves
5. there was no wind to sail the ship
6. she had sailed on the island pinnaces all her life

Lesson 2
Fill in the Blanks
1. respectable
2. realization
3. scowl
4. intimidated
5. gaudy
True and False
1. F
2. F
3. T
4. T
Multiple Choice
1. B
2. A
3. D
4. C
Who, What, Where, When, Why, and How
1. Kit's aunt and two cousins
2. she must fit herself to his ways
3. with Judith
4. he became sick and was never well again
5. she was afraid they might not tell her to come
6. the cornmeal has to be added to the boiling water a little pinch at a time

Lesson 3
Fill in the Blanks
1. pillory
2. reverent
3. duplicate
4 .allegiance
5. irresistible
True and False
1. T
2. T
3. T
4. F
Multiple Choice
1. A
2. C
3. B
4. D
Who, What, Where, When, Why, and How
1. Kit's grandfather
2. there should be no unclaimed land left in all of Hartford County
3. on the land his father gave him on his 16th birthday
4. twenty-five years ago
5. so the king's governor can't grant the land to his favorites
6. two

Lesson 4
Fill in the Blanks
1. menial
2. prickled
3. primer
4. obstreperous
5. cure
True and False
1. T
2. F
3. F
4. T
Multiple Choice
1. D
2. D
3. B
4. D
Who, What, Where, When, Why, and How
1. Mercy
2. a small wooden slab with a paper that has the alphabet and the Lord's Prayer
3. in the Great Meadow next to Blackbird Pond
4. the stories she herself enjoyed
5. she was wearing out her fine clothes scrubbing and cooking
6. it teaches the young children their letters and how to read and write their names, because they can't enter grammar school till they can read

Lesson 5
Fill in the Blanks
1. malicious
2. Quakers
3. branded
4. filigree
5. unfailing
True and False
1. T
2. F
3. F
4. T
Multiple Choice
1. D
2. B
3. C
4. A
Who, What, Where, When, Why, and How
1. Mr. Kimberley
2. blueberry cake and a kitten
3. it Kit's trunk it had been given to her by her grandfather
4. Mercy is in love with John
5. she is a Quaker
6. he said children are evil by nature and they have to be held with a firm hand

Lesson 6
Fill in the Blanks
1. mockery
2. scythe
3. loyalty
4. contagious
5. foreboding
True and False
1. T
2. T
3. F
4. T
Multiple Choice
1. A
2. C
3. B
4. D
Who, What, Where, When, Why, and How
1. John Holbrook
2. the autumn husking bee
3. to the soil he stands on
4. he wanted to ask for Mercy's hand in marriage
5. if he should hurt Judith, Mercy would never forgive him
6. they dipped the dangling wicks into tallow, hanged them to cool, dipped them again until the wax fattened

Lesson 7
Fill in the Blanks
1. buoyancy
2. distraction
3. commonwealths
4. dragoons
5. cavalier
True and False
1. T
2. T
3. F
4. F
Multiple Choice
1. C
2. A
3. D
4. C
Who, What, Where, When, Why, and How
1. William
2. it disappeared
3. in the middle of the table in plain sight of the council meeting
4. four days before Thanksgiving
5. he was unable to take his package because he was on another voyage
6. he held it in reverence as if it was priceless

Lesson 8
Fill in the Blanks
1. roistering
2. premonition
3. poultice
4. resolution
5. exhausted
True and False
1. T
2. T
3 .F
4. T
Multiple Choice
1. B
2. D
3. D
4. A
Who, What, Where, When, Why, and How
1. Hannah's
2. three sailors illuminated William Ashby's house with Jack-O-Lanterns
3. to join the militia in Massachusetts
4. a witch hunt they wanted to harm Hannah and Kit
5. the new governor is to declare all holidays when it pleases him
6. the little bud that was Prudence opened it's petals in the sunshine of Kit's friendship and Hanna's affection

Lesson 9
Fill in the Blanks
1. conscience
2. sustained
3. respectable
4. countenance
5. enchantments
True and False
1. T
2. T
3. T
4. F
Multiple Choice
1. D
2. A
3. B
4. C
Who, What, Where, When, Why, and How
1. the deacon of the church, the constable of the town, and Mr. and Mrs. Cruff
2. the little copy book with Prudence's name written over and over
3. in the shed behind his house
4. read the Good Book to him
5. Prudence is a witness to Kit's innocence
6. she was half starved, beaten and overworked, and not allowed to go to school

Lesson 10
Fill in the Blanks
1. curious
2. bygones
3. judged
4. intentions
5. governess
True and False
1. T
2. T
3. F
4. F
Multiple Choice
1. B
2. A
3. C
4. D
Who, What, Where, When, Why, and How
1. Nat
2. Nat is a sea captain with a ship of his own
3. where Nat was
4. early May
5. William wants Kit to forget her odd ways and fit in, Kit will not abandon her friends
6. seven

Made in the USA
Las Vegas, NV
03 September 2022